BULLEID LOCOMOTIVES
IN COLOUR

REX KENNEDY

IAN ALLAN
Publishing

First published 1993

ISBN 0 7110 2186 4

Published by Ian Allan Ltd, Shepperton, Surrey; and printed by Ian Allan Printing Ltd at its works at Coombelands in Runnymede, England.

Front cover:
Rebuilt 'West Country' class 4-6-2 No 34037 *Clovelly* is captured passing Queens Road, Battersea, with an 'additional' working – the down 18.14 Waterloo-Weymouth on 26 May 1967. No 34037 lasted in service until the end of Southern Region steam. *P. J. Lynch*

Back cover:
A 'Q1' class 0-6-0, No 33030, stands outside Feltham shed in June 1964. Feltham shed was opened in 1923 replacing Strawberry Hill which was converted for use by EMUs. *Geoff Rixon*

Right:
Two unrebuilt SR Bulleid Pacifics, both now preserved (No 35028 in its rebuilt state) pose for a picture. The two are seen in all their glory at Stewarts Lane shed on 15 June 1958. 'Merchant Navy' class 4-6-2 No 35028 *Clan Line*, nearest the camera, displays the 'Night Ferry' headboard while 'West Country' Pacific No 34092 carries the headboard of the 'Golden Arrow'. Stewarts Lane shed provided the motive power for both these prestige trains. By taking the Chatham route to Dover, the stock of the 'Night Ferry' worked right through from London to Paris using sleeping cars of the International Sleeping Car Co. This was one of the heaviest trains in Great Britain. The coaches were shortened versions of the Wagons-Lits standard Continental coaches to comply with SR loading gauge restrictions. The 'Golden Arrow' used British Pullman cars as far as Folkestone or Dover. *R. C. Riley*

Introduction

When Oliver Bulleid became Chief Mechanical Engineer of the Southern Railway in October 1937, his new employers considered that they had secured the services of one of Britain's most under-rated locomotive engineers. Having worked as Principal Assistant to the legendary Nigel Gresley since 1912, Bulleid had not only witnessed, but also made, significant contributions to some of the most praiseworthy locomotive designs in Britain. Bulleid was, however, a rather unusual choice for the Southern as his predecessor, Richard Maunsell, was forced to work under strict budgets and, consequently, had had little opportunity for experimentation. By complete contrast, Bulleid's reputation was that of an innovator who cared little for convention, and the Southern did not have to wait too long before seeing evidence of this.

Bulleid's maiden design for the Southern was that of the 'Merchant Navy' class 4-6-2 — the first type of Pacific locomotive to be built for that railway. Internally, the 'Merchant Navy' Pacifics included a number of tried-and-tested Gresley/Bulleid features such as the largest possible boiler, a wide firebox and three high-pressure cylinders driving the middle axle but, externally, the locomotives owed absolutely nothing to previous practices. Shrouded in an air-smoothed casing which, to Bulleid's disgust, was often referred to as 'stream-lining', the cosmetic appearance of the locomotives horrified the purists. Embarrassingly for Bulleid, revolutionary features, such as enclosing the chain-driven motion in an oil-bath, caused constant problems but, when the trouble spots were later redesigned, the 'Merchant Navy' Pacifics proved to be excellent engines.

The second Bulleid design for the Southern was the 'Q1' 0-6-0 and this class also raised countless eyebrows. Intent on producing a powerful 0-6-0 with the maximum size boiler and firebox, but keeping within a weight limit of 54 tons, Bulleid excluded every component which could possibly be discarded so as to minimise the weight. Naturally, many of the 'non-essential' fittings were those which contributed to the locomotive's cosmetic appearances and so the result was a highly-unorthodox looking machine. When it came to receiving criticism from traditionalists, however, Bulleid actually seemed to revel in it as the 'Charlies' (as the 'Q1s' were nicknamed) quickly became well-respected by the footplate crews and the operating department alike.

In 1945, a lightweight version of the 'Merchant Navy' appeared. This was the 'West Country' class, and these were augmented the following year by similar locomotives of the 'Battle of Britain' class. Once again, purists raised howls of protest at their cosmetic appearance but, when it came to doing the business, the locomotives happily operated over ground where no Pacifics had trodden before. They were used extensively on the lines westwards from Exeter to Plymouth, Ilfracombe, Padstow and, occasionally, Bude. Not so many years earlier, the suggestion that Pacifics would traverse these routes would have been met with roars of laughter. As if to emphasise the sheer versatility of the lightweight Pacifics, there were two instances in the 1950s of them working along the branch to Sidmouth — a line that had usually been worked by 0-4-4Ts since the year dot. In common with the 'Merchant Navy' 4-6-2s, a number of the lightweight Pacifics were later rebuilt without their air-smoothed casing although, by the time the rebuilding programme started in 1956, Bulleid had long-since left Eastleigh. However, the rebuilt versions are included in this book to complete the story of Bulleid's locomotives.

Bulleid's final steam locomotive design for the Southern Railway was the 'Leader' class and, while his earlier designs might have been considered unorthodox, his Pacifics and 'Q1s' positively smacked of convention when compared to his latest foray into the future. The revolutionary design of the 'Leader' prompted the comment from one observer of the day that Bulleid 'seemed as if he were trying to re-invent the steam locomotive'. As history shows, the 'Leaders' were a failure and, although one actually carried out trials, it never entered revenue-earning service.

Having a keen eye for innovation, it was not only steam locomotive design which kept Bulleid busy, as two of his mixed traffic Co-Co electric locomotives were built at Ashford, one in 1941 and the other in 1943. They went on to have long and useful lives including, from May 1949, command of the Victoria-Newhaven boat trains. A third member of the class was completed by BR in 1948. Furthermore, a pair of 1Co-Co1 diesel-electric locomotives were ordered by Bulleid from the English Electric Co late in 1947 (with another following later) and designs were prepared for a 500hp diesel-mechanical shunter. However, neither type was delivered until after Nationalisation. An unsung aspect of Bulleid's work involved the upgrading of older designs; the fitting of multiple-jet blastpipes and larger chimneys to the 'Lord Nelson' class 4-6-0s was one of his greatest successes.

In September 1949, Bulleid took early retirement from the Southern Region but, rather than enjoy traditional leisure pursuits, he went to work in a consultative capacity for Coras Iompair Eireann,

the Irish Transport Co. In December 1957, *Trains Illustrated* quietly reported: 'Mr Bulleid's turf-burning prototype locomotive for the CIE emerged from Inchicore Works. . . no one seems yet to have penetrated the security barrier to obtain a photograph. . . An external family resemblance to the 'Leader' is apparent. . . '. Mr Bulleid was far from finished.

Sadly, Oliver Bulleid is often remembered more for his extravagances than his successes. He constantly upset traditionalists, not only with his designs, but even in smaller aspects such as the adoption of a Continental-style numbering scheme for his new locomotives. As for the Southern Railway's distinctive Malachite Green livery, that was a Bulleid innovation as well. With the benefit of hindsight it has often been remarked that, while Bulleid was in the chair at Eastleigh, the standard of pre-

Below:
The first of Bulleid's unusually-designed Pacific locomotives of the 'Merchant Navy' class, with the 'air-smoothed' casing, for the Southern Railway were completed in November 1940 but, due to war effort commitments at Eastleigh, construction of the tenders had to be taken on by Ashford Works. Eventually, the first member of the class, No 21C1, left the erecting shops at Eastleigh to be steamed in the yard on 17 February 1941. The next day it worked to Winchester and, on 22 February, hauled 10 coaches from Bournemouth West. No 21C1 was named *Channel Packet* after the cross-Channel fleet of the Southern Railway. The numbering system denoted 4-6-2 (the wheel arrangement — the six coupled wheels being denoted by the letter 'C'), and the first two figures denoting the number of leading and trailing axles. The initial duties of the locomotive on freight and semi-fast passenger work in April and May 1941 were modified by modification and adjustment work at Eastleigh Works. Carrying its BR number, 35001, which it received in October 1949, *Channel Packet* is pictured at Stewarts Lane shed on 10 May 1959, bearing the BR Green livery and with the modified 5,000gall tender. Bulleid's air-smoothed Pacifics were fitted with chain-driven valve-gear which was totally enclosed in an oil bath. Rebuilding of this locomotive was completed in August 1959 and No 35001 was withdrawn in November 1964, its final allocation being Bournemouth. *R. C. Riley*

sentation and maintenance of the Southern's locomotives and rolling stock was impeccable, but perhaps that was an automatic side-effect of having such a high-profile Chief Mechanical Engineer.

Certainly, without doubt, the memorable locomotive designs of Oliver Bulleid have inspired railway preservationists to restore as many examples as is humanly possible. Eleven of his air-smoothed designed locomotives are now back in circulation. These, and many of the rebuilt versions, give a great deal of pleasure to railway enthusiasts all over Britain, and provide impressive motive power on main line steam runs and a great deal of interest at preservation sites. Even one of the 'Q1' 0-6-0s was saved as a reminder of his unusual designs. Nothing but praise and admiration must go to the many preservationists, young and old, who have made all this possible with their hard work and determination to preserve an important part of railway history.

Rex Kennedy May 1993

Left:
The nameplate of No 35001 *Channel Packet* seen in September 1957. It displays the shipping company's flag with the letters SR denoting Southern Railway. The company flags were displayed on the nameplates and these attractive and elaborate 'Merchant Navy' class plates became much sought after by collectors as locomotives were withdrawn, and commanded vast sums of money. *R. C. Riley*

Right:
Over the years, there was a variety of liveries applied to the 'Merchant Navy' Pacifics. One of the more unusual was dark blue, which was the livery adopted by BR for express passenger locomotives. This livery was used on No 35024 *East Asiatic Company*, as seen here, and on No 35026 *Lamport & Holt Line*. The blue livery was applied to No 35024 when the locomotive received a 6,000gall tender, in February 1949. Its earlier tender, to which it had been attached since entering traffic in November 1948, passed to 'Battle of Britain' light Pacific No 34089 *602 Squadron*. Nos 35024 and 35026 were the only two members of the class never to be painted in the Malachite Green livery. In this view, the standard blue livery with black & white lining is clearly visible as No 35024 *East Asiatic Company*, with polished rods, is seen at Waterloo with her train of SR green stock. The train also includes a Pullman car for the use of HRH Princess Elizabeth on her visit to Weymouth.
The Late S. C. Townroe/Colour-Rail BRS307

Left:
In April 1949, prior to the standard blue livery with black & white lining being applied, 'Merchant Navy' Pacific No 35024 *East Asiatic Company* carried red stripes on the blue background but this variant lasted for only a few days. This rare photograph shows the locomotive in this striking livery. The majority of the Bulleid Pacifics entered service with nameplates boarded up, as seen here, until an official naming ceremony took place. *The Late S. C. Townroe/Colour-Rail BRS306*

Above right:
With a down express, 'Merchant Navy' Pacific No 35001 *Channel Packet* heads south having just emerged from Weald Tunnel in Kent in 1955. During its life, this locomotive completed 1,095,884 miles in service. No 35001 is seen with its unmodified 5,000gall tender — modifications taking place in June 1956 entailing the removal of some of the top plating above tank level. This eased coaling, watering and vision when reversing, all of which pleased the footplatemen. Following the fracturing at speed of an axle on 'Merchant Navy' Pacific No 35020 *Bibby Line*, on 24 April 1953, when hauling a Waterloo to Exeter express, the entire class of 'Merchant Navy' Pacifics was withdrawn for ultrasonic testing of coupled axles, resulting in faults being found on No 35001 *Channel Packet*, and also on Nos 35002, 35023 and 35024. Axles were also replaced on Nos 35025 and 35026 as a precaution. While testing took place, duties were taken over by ex-LMS and BR Class 5 4-6-0s, ex-LNER 'V2s' and 'B1s' and 'Britannia' Pacifics. The first 'Merchant Navy' returned to traffic on 16 May 1953.
P. M. Alexander/Colour-Rail BRS467

Below right:
From May 1958 to December 1961, the self-weighing tender, introduced in May 1952 and first fitted to 'Merchant Navy' Pacific No 35012 *United States Lines*, was attached to 'Merchant Navy' No 35024 *East Asiatic Company*. The modification of this tender was for trials to determine fuel and water consumption, and this also entailed cutting away part of the top plating. The self-weighing tender is seen attached to No 35024 in this scene at Nine Elms shed, under the coaling tower in May 1958 and, prior to the tender being used with this locomotive, it also ran with Nos 35018, 35014 and 35015. Once no longer required, in December 1961, the self-weighing equipment was removed and a new body was fitted to the tender chassis. *R. C. Riley*

Left:

In March 1942 the first of the unique Bulleid 'Q1' class 0-6-0s entered service. The 40 members of the class had been recommended by Bulleid as long ago as August 1940, when it became apparent that powerful freight locomotives, with a wide route availability, were required. At first, two-cylinder 2-6-0s were recommended but 0-6-0s won the day as these were more economical to build and provided better adhesion. Due to a delay, it was mid-1941 before parts were available for construction to be carried out at Ashford and Brighton. Following the Bulleid tradition of using the letter 'C' for locomotives with six coupled wheels, these locomotives were numbered C1 to C40. The whole batch was constructed in the nine months from March to December 1942. BR gave these locomotives the power classification '5F' and renumbered them 33001-33040. At Factory Junction, Battersea, No 33027 heads a down freight on 23 August 1958. For many years during the 1950s this locomotive was a resident of Feltham shed, and it was one of the last three 'Q1' 0-6-0s to be withdrawn, in January 1966, and was sent later that year to Newport, Gwent where it was broken up by the contractors, Buttigiegs. *R. C. Riley*

Below left:

The stark appearance of these 'Utility' 0-6-0 'Q1' class locomotives was partly due to the saving of expense and time in construction, but the excellent cylinders on these locomotives allowed high mileage in service, and only seven sets required renewing before withdrawal. Livery was black from day one and No 33015 shows off this livery to its best advantage as it gleams in the sun at Nine Elms on 6 September 1958. No 33015 was one of the 20 members of the class to be built at Brighton. *R. C. Riley*

Right:

With locomotives simmering away below at Stewarts Lane depot, 'Q1' 0-6-0 No 33038 passes with empty coaching stock off the 'Bournemouth Belle' express on 10 May 1959. These remarkable locomotives, although initially built for heavy freight work with the impending transfer of more freight from the roads after World War 2, could be found on a variety of duties including empty stock workings of this nature and even passenger work over the Southern's many branch lines.
R. C. Riley

Left:
On 11 August 1963, 'Q1' 0-6-0 No 33036 is pictured near the coaling stage at Guildford shed, its home depot for the last three years of its life. As tender-first working provided difficulties regarding drivers' controls, Bulleid actually fitted additional controls on the right-hand side in the cab of this locomotive when num-bered C36, in 1945, and also gave it a 'West Country' tender to improve vision. These adaptations were removed in May 1946, since they proved to be of no advantage. *R. C. Riley*

Above:
A down parcels train, hauled by 'Q1' 0-6-0 No 33020, is pictured passing through Barnes, heading towards Chiswick & Grove Park, in November 1965. By this time, only three members of this class were still in ser-vice, all of which ended their working life operating from Guildford shed. *J. B. Snell/Colour-Rail*

Above:

The first of Bulleid's light Pacifics entered service in May 1945 and were named after West Country towns and landmarks. Following his numbering scheme used on the 'Merchant Navy' Pacifics and 'Q1' 0-6-0s, Bulleid commenced the numbering sequence of the 'West Country' class from 21C101. By Nationalisation, 70 of these light Pacifics had been constructed and, from No 21C149, had been named after RAF Squadrons, airfields, etc, associated with the Battle of Britain and were termed 'Battle of Britain' class. There was structurally no difference between these two classes of Bulleid light Pacifics. Of the 110 locomotives which made up these two classes, 50 did not have their air-smoothed casing removed. British Railways continued the building programme of this type in 1948. The first to emerge after Nationalisation was No 34071, in April 1948. Sporting Bulleid's Malachite Green livery, one of the BR-built 'Battle of Britain' class light Pacifics, No 34083, later to be named *605 Squadron*, prepares to depart from Victoria station, in April 1949, with the prestigious 'Golden Arrow' service. *J. M. Jarvis/Colour-Rail BRS196*

Right:

No 34002 *Salisbury*, numbered 21C102 until November 1948, seen here at Exeter in July 1960, came into service in June 1945 and was never rebuilt. The locomotive survived until the last year of steam operation on the Southern Region, 1967, and spent its last years in service running from Nine Elms shed. It had previously spent a number of years at Exmouth Junction operating trains to Ilfracombe and Plymouth. *Geoff Rixon*

Above:
When Bulleid decided he needed a more powerful locomotive for use in the West Country it was not originally
anticipated that this would eventually be of a 4-6-2
wheel arrangement. However, more locomotives were
also required for the Eastern Section to operate on services from Victoria as the electrification programme
had been suspended due to the outbreak of war. With
the Eastern Section requirements taking priority, the
Bulleid light Pacifics went into production but it was
felt in certain circles that, particularly for West Country
routes, Bulleid was producing a giant to do a man's job.
Working in the West Country, with an up freight, near

Whimple, No 34030 *Watersmeet* includes condemned
coaches in its train, in August 1964. This is another
member of the class which was never rebuilt.
Alan Sainty Collection/Colour-Rail BRS680

Right:
Bulleid 'West Country' class Pacific No 34039
Boscastle was also a Southern-built locomotive, emerg-
ing as 21C139 in September 1946 from Brighton
Works. Rebuilt in January 1959, this locomotive was
one of the many that ended up at Woodham's scrapyard
in Barry Docks, where it lay rotting for over seven
years. *Boscastle* and many of its companions in that

South Wales graveyard have now been preserved,
whilst others are in the course of restoration, thanks to
the work of many hard-working volunteers. Prior to
being rebuilt, No 34039 *Boscastle* is pictured leaving
Southampton in 1957 with a Brighton-Bournemouth
train. Note the extended deflectors fitted to this locomotive. No 34039 was the first of the Bulleid light Pacifics
to receive, on 3 August 1949, the Brunswick Green livery with orange & black lining. Alongside, in this
scene, beneath the signal gantry, stands 'Lord Nelson'
No 30856 *Lord St Vincent*.
The Late B. J. Swain/Colour-Rail BRS428

Above:
In January 1947, Southern 'Battle of Britain' light Pacific No 21C154 *Lord Beaverbrook* entered service. It received its BR number, 34054, in March 1949. In this 1959 view No 34054 is seen in gleaming ex-works condition at Eastleigh sporting the Brunswick Green livery. This locomotive was one of three members of the class, together with *Spitfire* and *Hurricane* to be named at a ceremony at Waterloo station on 16 Septem-ber 1947. Lord Beaverbrook, who was Minister of Air-craft Production during the war, unveiled his own nameplate and coat of arms.
The Late B. J. Swain/Colour-Rail BRS 780

Right:
On 19 July 1956, 'Battle of Britain' Pacific No 34057 *Biggin Hill* coasts along the sea wall at Teignmouth in Devon with the 11.35am Exeter-Plymouth train. This was one of a selection of 'Battle of Britain' Pacifics to carry the RAF insignia. In fact, during overhaul at East-leigh Works in September 1960, the oval RAF insignia plates were removed from No 34068 *Kenley* and were inadvertently refitted to No 34058 *Sir Frederick Pile*, No 34068 receiving that locomotive's oval plate. How-ever, they were not changed back to how they should have been and it is believed that both locomotives car-ried the wrong 'ovals' until withdrawn. *R. C. Riley*

Below:
Another Southern Railway-built 'Battle of Britain' light Pacific, No 34061 *73 Squadron*, certainly looks as if it has been in the Battle of Britain in this view of it at Eastleigh in June 1963. However, this allows us to see clearly what lay beneath the air-smoothed casing. Completed in April 1947, this locomotive was never rebuilt.

No 34061 was one of the few members of the class to be broken up at Woods of Queenborough, Kent. *Geoff Rixon*

Right:
Watching the Bulleid Pacifics arrive at and depart from Barnstaple over the curving river bridge was always a wonderful sight as trains crossed the River Taw here *en route* to Barnstaple Town station and the north Devon resort of Ilfracombe. On 16 June 1962, 'Battle of Britain' Pacific No 34066 *Spitfire*, overdue for a repaint, is seen at this location. *R. C. Riley*

Left:
In May 1964, and now looking in excellent condition, 'Battle of Britain' light Pacific No 34066 *Spitfire* is seen climbing towards Honiton with a down express. This was another locomotive to carry the RAF insignia on an oval plaque below the nameplate. On 30 May 1958 this locomotive worked the first Glasgow-Eastbourne car sleeper over Southern Region metals. This duty was later a turn for a Battersea-based Pacific.
The Late A. E. R. Cope/Colour-Rail BRS182

Right:
The nameplate, which was fitted to the unrebuilt 'Battle of Britain' light Pacific No 34066 *Spitfire*, illustrates the RAF insignia and pale blue background to the nameplate and the crest. This locomotive was never rebuilt.
Geoff Rixon

21

Above:
One of the last 'Battle of Britain' light Pacifics to be constructed by the Southern Railway was No 21C167 *Tangmere* (later No 34067), which entered service in September 1947. This locomotive was one of the many Bulleid Pacifics to escape the cutter's torch having been, with many others, retrieved from Woodham's scrapyard at Barry Docks. In this fascinating North Devon scene, No 34067 *Tangmere* is pictured near Hunter's Inn, with a Barnstaple to Ilfracombe train, being banked by 'N' class Mogul No 31856, tender-first! *P. W. Gray/Colour-Rail BRS200*

Right:
Double-headed unrebuilt 'Battle of Britain' light Pacifics, No 34075 *264 Squadron* (BR-built) and No 34069 *Hawkinge* (SR-built), bring the 2.55pm Ilfracombe-Waterloo train past the reservoir about a mile up the bank from Hunter's Inn. This was a delightful line to watch these light Pacifics at work and the ideal place for the railway photographer to capture these fine locomotives in a pleasing rural environment. *P. W. Gray/Colour-Rail BRS202*

Left:
The locomotives used on the 'Golden Arrow' duty were always turned out immaculately by Stewarts Lane men and this is clearly seen by this view of BR-built 'West Country' Pacific No 34091 *Weymouth,* which is being prepared to take out this prestige train on 22 October 1957. This locomotive was the only Bulleid Pacific not to complete half a million miles in service, achieving only 469,073 miles. It was the last 'West Country' class Pacific to be named at an official ceremony, on 29 December 1949. *R. C. Riley*

Above:
In June 1955, a gleaming unrebuilt 'West Country' Pacific, No 34095 *Brentor,* takes on water at Southampton Central when hauling an up express for Waterloo. No 34095 was one of the six Bulleid light Pacifics which were built at Eastleigh and not at Brighton. This locomotive never carried a shield similar to most of the other 'West Country' Pacifics. The scroll, denoting the locomotive class; was fitted 12in below the nameplate on the unrebuilt version of No 34095 but on the rebuilt version it was directly under the nameplate.
The Late B. J. Swain/Colour-Rail BRS856

Exmouth Junction shed, on 9 June 1963, and two Bulleid light Pacifics await their next call to duty. Taking pride of place is 'West Country' No 34106 *Lydford*, one of the last of the class to be built by BR (in March 1950) and, ironically, one of the first to be withdrawn (in September 1964), having never been rebuilt. At the time, Exmouth Junction had an allocation of around 30 Bulleid Pacifics. *Norman Glover*

'West Country' Pacific No 34023 *Blackmore Vale* was used on a LCGB Railtour over the Swanage branch on 7 May 1967, two months before being taken out of BR service. The train is seen at Corfe Castle station carrying the headboard 'Dorset Coast Express'. Until April 1950, the spelling on the nameplate of this locomotive read *Blackmoor Vale*. The locomotive was preserved on withdrawal and has now been in private ownership for more than 25 years. *Norman Glover*

Below:

Bulleid's last design for the Southern Railway was the controversial 0-6-6-0T 'Leader' class. However, the locomotives of this unusual type did not appear until 1949. Of the three members of the class built, only one reached trials stage. The firebox was sited in the centre of the locomotive and the heat generated from this area made it unbearable for the fireman to work. In this rare colour photograph of the only 'Leader' to undertake trials, No 36001 is being painted in a grey livery in East-leigh Works yard in June 1949 — the lining and numbers still have to be applied.

The Late S. C. Townroe/Colour-Rail BRS331

Right:

Another of Bulleid's contributions to railway engineering was his turf-burning locomotive — the mixed traffic 0-6-6-0T introduced in 1957 for the Coras Iompair Eireaan (CIE). The idea came to Bulleid as Eire had vast amounts of peat, or turf, but had to import coal.

However, four times more turf than coal was required to produce the same quantity of heat. Due to the shortage of fuel created by the war, turf continued to be used in briquette form. Even when the CIE's fleet of locomotives turned to diesel, Bulleid was still insistent that turf-burning was necessary as a standby, in case of an oil crisis. In this view, turf-burner No CC1 is seen wearing a fresh coat of grey paint, in 1957, when on trial at Rathfarnham.

National Railway Museum/Colour-Rail IR198

Left:
The rebuilding programme on the 'Merchant Navy' Pacifics commenced in February 1956 with No 35018 *British India Line*. Just three months after the conversion, this locomotive is seen at Waterloo awaiting departure with the 'Bournemouth Belle'. Beside the 'Belle' in the bay is No 35020 *Bibby Line*. This locomotive had only been rebuilt during the previous month. Both of these impressive giants are in immaculate condition and display their Brunswick Green lined livery to good effect. Both were originally constructed by the Southern Railway in 1945.
The Late B. J. Swain/Colour-Rail BRS375

Above right:
During 1959, rebuilt 'Merchant Navy' Pacific No 35015 *Rotterdam Lloyd* was the only member of the class allocated to Stewarts Lane and was used on the prestige 'Golden Arrow', so it was a bonus for the railway enthusiast at a time when 'Battle of Britain' and 'West Country' Pacifics were generally found on this train. On 21 March 1959, in immaculate condition, this locomotive, with British and French flags in position, was captured at Stewarts Lane waiting to take up its 'Golden Arrow' duty. *R. C. Riley*

Below right:
A morning West of England express, hauled by rebuilt 'Merchant Navy' Pacific No 35005 *Canadian Pacific*, another early rebuild, is seen at Axminster in June 1959. Later it was to spend its last years in BR service working from Bournemouth and Weymouth sheds. Originally constructed in 1941 and not rebuilt until May 1959, this locomotive was the only member of the class built before 1945 not to complete one million miles in service. *N. L. Browne*

Left:
Having completed its run to Folkestone with the 'Golden Arrow' on 4 April 1959, Stewarts Lane's sole 'Merchant Navy' Pacific, No 35015 *Rotterdam Lloyd* takes on coal at Folkestone Junction shed. Also in attendance is 'R1' class 0-6-0T No 31107. These tank locomotives were used for hauling the 'Golden Arrow' Pullman stock from Folkestone Harbour station to Folkestone Junction. *R. C. Riley*

Above:
Prior to the electrification of the ex-L&SWR main line from Waterloo to Bournemouth, the Bulleid Pacifics reigned supreme over this route and enthusiasts would spend hours beside the line watching a variety of these powerful giants rush by at regular intervals. But there was no finer a sight than that of a Bulleid Pacific on the 'Bournemouth Belle' with a set of Pullman cars in tow. In February 1962, rebuilt 'Merchant Navy' Pacific

No 35029 *Ellerman Lines* is pictured between Hampton Court Junction and Esher with a down 'Bournemouth Belle'. This locomotive can now be seen in a sectioned form in the National Railway Museum. *Geoff Rixon*

Left:

Originally, the nameplates fitted to the rebuilt 'Merchant Navy' Pacific, *Ellerman Lines* had a red background, as seen, but during BR days some backgrounds were repainted black. The letters of the shipping lines on these nameplates were 3in high by ½in wide and raised ¼in. The words MERCHANT NAVY CLASS had letters 2⅝in high by $\frac{7}{16}$in wide, and these were raised $\frac{3}{16}$in. The plates were cast in gunmetal.
Geoff Rixon

Below left:

On 30 July 1961, the 4.00pm Sunday service from Waterloo to Plymouth, headed by 'Merchant Navy' Pacific No 35013 *Blue Funnel*, nears the village of Barford St Martin, between Wilton and Dinton. Built by the Southern Railway as 21C13, this locomotive was named *Blue Funnel Line* at a ceremony at Waterloo station on 17 April 1945 but, by July of that year, new nameplates had be fitted and the word 'Line' had been dropped and its place on the bottom half of the circular nameplate had been taken up by the words *Certum Pete Finem* — a Latin phrase which means 'make a good job of it' — and it regularly did! *Hugh Ballantyne*

Right:

BR-built Bulleid 'Merchant Navy' Pacific No 35024 *East Asiatic Company* was, for many years, a resident of Exmouth Junction, but when many of these locomotives ended their days at Weymouth towards the end of steam on the Southern Region, the locomotive spent its last days at the latter shed. The impressive gantry at Southampton Central station always seemed to be a favourite location for railway photographers to 'frame' their subjects and No 35024 is pictured here awaiting departure from this location with its train for Bournemouth in April 1962.
G. W. Parry Collection/Colour-Rail BRS472

Above:
An unusual view of Waterloo station taken from the 'Atlantic Coast Express' on 16 May 1964. The famous train was being hauled by 'Merchant Navy' Pacific No 35029 *Ellerman Lines* on this occasion. Awaiting departure with an express is another 'Merchant Navy', No 35018 *British India Line*, which was, in February 1956, the first member of the class to be rebuilt. Another rebuilt Pacific can be seen in the background. *Norman Glover*

Right:
The scene is Sidmouth Junction, and rebuilt 'Merchant Navy' Pacific No 35009 *Shaw Savill* comes to a halt with a down train from Waterloo in June 1964. The connecting diesel unit for the coastal resort of Sidmouth sits in the bay. Prior to the closure of the East Devon branches between 1965 and 1967, the quiet seaside resorts of the area were well served by connecting services from London and Exeter. *Geoff Rixon*

In August 1964, rebuilt 'Merchant Navy' Pacific No 35030 *Elder Dempster Lines* departs from Southampton with the down 'Bournemouth Belle' and passes under the splendid (now sadly demolished and much lamented) signal gantry at this location. It was initially intended to name this class of locomotive after World War 2 British battle victories but, as the class was introduced in 1941, there had been few successes by this time and the idea was abandoned. Even capital cities of Commonwealth countries were considered. However, the naming of locomotives of this class after shipping lines which used Southampton was suggested by the Chairman of the Union Castle Line and was eventually adopted. *M. Chapman/Colour-Rail BRS308*

Right:
Waterloo station, pictured in September 1964, and rebuilt 'Merchant Navy' Pacific No 35014 *Nederland Line* blows off steam while standing at the platform. For many years a Nine Elms engine, No 35014 survived almost to the end of steam on the Southern Region, although latterly the locomotive was based at Weymouth — the last outpost for these popular locomotives. *N. L. Browne*

Above:
This illustration shows clearly the black background that was applied to some of the 'Merchant Navy' name-plates in BR days. The plate which was affixed to No 35014 *Nederland Line* is portrayed here.
Geoff Rixon

Right:
Another Waterloo view shows 'Merchant Navy' Pacific No 35030 awaiting departure for Bournemouth in September 1964. Although this locomotive survived to the end of steam on the Southern Region, it was not one of the 11 members of the class to be saved for preservation. *N. L. Browne*

Above:
Although by the end of steam on the Southern Region the Bulleid Pacifics were looking in a sorry state, in the mid-1960s they were generally always turned out immaculately, since they were the pride and joy of the men at the depots. This September 1964 scene captured at Woking shows rebuilt 'Merchant Navy' No 35008 *Orient Line* pulling away with a train for Exeter in its gleaming Brunswick Green livery. This locomotive completed 1,286,418 miles in service, the second highest mileage for a Bulleid Pacific. This was only exceeded by No 35007 *Aberdeen Commonwealth* which travelled 1,318,765 miles. *Geoff Rixon*

Right:
In June 1964, the down 'Bournemouth Belle' speeds through the cutting on the approach to Weybridge with the full rake of chocolate & cream Pullman cars in tow. In charge is rebuilt 'Merchant Navy' Pacific No 35020 *Bibby Line*. In June 1945 this was the last member of the class to be completed by the Southern Railway. The first BR-built 'Merchant Navy' Pacific, No 35021 *New Zealand Line*, was not completed until September 1948. *Geoff Rixon*

Above:

Looking its immaculate best, 'Merchant Navy' Pacific No 35028 *Clan Line* heads south-west and approaches Esher with a down Bournemouth special in September 1966. On the many occasions when this now famous locomotive has turned out on main-line steam runs since the end of BR steam, it has always looked an impressive sight. No 35028 was one of the seven members of the class to survive until July 1967 and the end of steam on the Southern Region. It was, however, the only one of the seven to survive into preservation. This view clearly shows the advantages which were obtained when the original Bulleid tenders were cut down to help with vision when reversing. *Geoff Rixon*

Right:

Rebuilt 'Merchant Navy' Pacific No 35028 *Clan Line* approaches Wimbledon, on 14 June 1967, with the 6.54pm Waterloo-Salisbury evening train. A Southern Class 4EPB unit, No 5022, heads up the main line towards Waterloo. To the left, Southern Class 4SUB unit No 4742 also approaches Wimbledon station from the direction of the depot. A typical Southern scene of the 1950s and 1960s. *C. J. Gammell*

A selection of nameplates which have appeared on rebuilt 'Merchant Navy' Pacifics. The plates for *Lamport & Holt Line*, *Peninsular & Oriental S. N. Co.* and *Port Line*, photographed by *Geoff Rixon*, all carry the red background, but the background colour of the *Cunard White Star* nameplate, photographed on 6 September 1958 by *R. C. Riley*, is black. *Peninsular & Oriental S. N. Co.* was the first nameplate to be fitted with 3in high letters instead of letters 4⅜in high, which were fitted to eight of the first batch of 'Merchant Navy' Pacifics. It was also one of three members of the class to have the flag flying in the same direction on both sides of the locomotive.

Left:
Travelling through appropriate countryside, rebuilt 'West Country' Pacific No 34024 *Tamar Valley* bursts out of the tunnel near Tavistock North with an up express on 7 July 1961. At this time, there were around 36 Bulleid Pacifics allocated to Exmouth Junction for working trains over ex-L&SWR routes in the West Country, proving their usefulness over these 'Withered Arm' routes. *R. C. Riley*

Above:
On 18 May 1964, 'West Country' Pacific No 34017 *Ilfracombe* is pictured at Basingstoke. When steam traction largely disappeared in Kent in 1961, with the last regular steam-hauled boat train and the last steam-hauled 'Golden Arrow', a total of 16 Bulleid Pacifics were transferred to Nine Elms, Bournemouth, Salisbury and Eastleigh sheds. No 34017 was one of the seven which went to Nine Elms and, by this time, was regularly used on the 'Bournemouth Belle'. *Norman Glover*

Below:

In September 1964, an Exeter-Waterloo train approaches Woking from the west hauled by 'West Country' Pacific No 34010 *Sidmouth*. This locomotive was withdrawn from service in March 1965 when allocated to Eastleigh and six months later was taken to Barry Docks for scrapping. Fortunately, it was saved by the preservationists for future restoration and is currently based at Middlesbrough, well away from its tra-ditional stamping grounds. The green coaching stock often hauled by the Bulleid Pacifics, as seen in this view, was a delight to see in the last years of steam, reminding us of better days on the Southern.
Geoff Rixon

Right:

The 1.30pm Waterloo-Bournemouth working approaches Worting Junction, near Basingstoke, on 19 June 1965. In charge is 'West Country' No 34101 *Hartland* — an Eastleigh-allocated engine. This is another locomotive which was saved from the cutter's torch after rotting away at Woodham's scrapyard in Barry for nearly 12 years. Like *Sidmouth*, this locomotive is now based well away from Southern Region metals, this time in Leicestershire where restoration work was recently completed. *C. J. Gammell*

Above:
Rebuilt 'Battle of Britain' Pacific No 34056 *Croydon* passes Esher with a four-coach train for Basingstoke on 30 April 1966. During its last five years in service, No 34056 was a Salisbury engine. Salisbury was a depot which kept its steam allocation right up to the end of steam on the Southern Region in 1967. *Geoff Rixon*

Right:
Passing beneath Battledown flyover, near Basingstoke which carries the up Bournemouth-Waterloo line at Worting Junction over the line to Yeovil, is rebuilt 'Battle of Britain' Pacific No 34089 *602 Squadron*, with a down Salisbury train. As with the 'West Country' Pacifics, the coat of arms on the 'Squadrons' was carried above the nameplate on the rebuilt versions, but below the nameplate on the original unrebuilt locomotive. *P. J. Hughes/Colour-Rail BRS699*

Above:
On 18 March 1967, during the last year of steam on the Southern Region, 'West Country' Pacific No 34047 *Callington* is caught by the late afternoon sun near Weybridge. The locomotive is seen with the 4.15pm Feltham-Eastleigh freight. Rebuilt 'West Country' and 'Battle of Britain' Pacifics were now down to about 30,

but many of them were still looking in reasonable condition. *C. J. Gammell*

Right:
By the spring of 1967, certain of the Bulleid Pacifics were starting to lose their nameplates, one of the most attractive features of these locomotives, and, on

18 March 1967, 'West Country' No 34100 *Appledore* was seen in this state. It heads a down Bournemouth train through Raynes Park with a glimmer of its lined Brunswick Green livery peeping through. The Bournemouth electrification scheme was now complete and the inauguration of the new service was to coincide with the final withdrawal of SR steam. *F. Hornby*

Left:
By June 1967, 'West Country' Pacific No 34013
Okehampton had also lost its nameplate and the days
were numbered for scenes of this nature, as this locomotive is seen with a freight near Worgret Junction,
Wareham, between Bournemouth and Weymouth.
Somehow, Bulleid Pacifics on freight trains did not
seem right. Still, all the powerful passenger locomotives such as ex-LMS 'Duchesses', 'Britannias',
ex-LNER 'A4s' and Great Western 'Castles' were all

relegated to these menial tasks in their dying years.
R. C. Riley

Above:
Steam on the Southern was now drawing to a close and
sights such as this would soon be no more as fielders in
a cricket match on Wimbledon Common catch a brief
glance of the 6.43pm Waterloo-Southampton boat train
on 14 June 1967. In charge is No 34090 *Sir Eustace
Missenden, Southern Railway*, the Bulleid Pacific

named after the General Manager of the Southern Railway during the war. The naming of this locomotive at
Waterloo on 15 February 1948 created more interest
than any of the other naming ceremonies. It was said
that this was not only a tribute to the man himself, but
also to the 67,000 Southern Railway employees who
worked long hours during the war when constantly
under air attack. This locomotive's nameplate indicated
that it was a member of the 'Battle of Britain' class.
C. J. Gammell

Above:
The last Friday of steam on the Southern Region, 7 July 1967, saw rebuilt 'West Country' Pacific No 34025 *Whimple* on the 6.54pm Waterloo-Yeovil train. This well-patronised train, which was to be expected, is pictured at Vauxhall, soon after leaving Waterloo, and the locomotive is sadly devoid of nameplates. When constructed in its original state, with its air-smoothed casing, in March 1946, this locomotive was numbered 21C125 but, between 11 April and 23 April 1948, it was named *Rough Tor*. The name *Whimple* was not applied until 3 May 1948. *R. C. Riley*

Right:
Minus its nameplates, but in reasonable condition, rebuilt 'Battle of Britain' Pacific No 34052 *Lord Dowding* trundles through Basingstoke station with a freight on 7 July 1967, just one day before steam ended for good on the Southern Region. Although there looks plenty of life left in this impressive machine, it was destined for Cashmore's scrapyard at Newport, where it was broken up in March 1968. *Lord Dowding* was one of the three members of the 'Battle of Britain' class to be named at Waterloo station on 11 September 1947, the seventh anniversary of the Battle of Britain. The three locomotives — Nos 21C152 *Lord Dowding*, 21C151 *Winston Churchill* and 21C164 *Fighter Command* — all lined up at platform No 11 and Lord Dowding himself, Marshal of the Royal Air Force, carried out the unveiling. An RAF band was also in attendance. In 1962, *Fighter Command* was fitted with the experimental Giesl ejector system. This replaced the Bulleid blastpipe and chimney, and successfully reduced the problems of sparks being thrown from the chimney. *Norman Glover*

LAUNCESTON

WEST COUNTRY CLASS

A selection of nameplates carried by members of the 'West Country' class. Three of them, which were affixed to rebuilt versions *Launceston*, *Exeter* and *Honiton*, carry their coats of arms above the nameplate but, on the unrebuilt versions, as shown by the nameplate of *Tavistock*, the coat of arms is carried below the nameplate and the background colour is black. *R. C. Riley (2), Geoff Rixon (2)*

Left:
In 1951, the first of Bulleid's express diesel-electric locomotives entered service and was numbered No 10201. The power unit was the English Electric 1,750 bhp 16SVT engine which had improved greatly in performance between Bulleid's initial discussion with English Electric, four years earlier, and the construction of the locomotive. A 1Co-Co1 wheel arrangement was adopted and trials with this locomotive commenced in November 1950. During 1951, No 10201 was tested for a time on the St Pancras-Derby line. After repainting it was placed on display at the 'Festival of Britain'. In its livery of black with a silver waistband, No 10201 is seen in the bay at Dorchester South station with an up train.
The Late S. C. Townroe/Colour-Rail DE628

Below left:
Bulleid diesel-electric No 10202 also emerged in 1951. As the intention was to use the type in multiple, gangway connections were fitted to each end of locomotives 10201 and 10202. Coupled with No 10201, this locomotive worked the 'Royal Scot' for a while. No 10202 was also tried out on the 'Golden Arrow' and 'Night Ferry' in 1954 and one could say that the experience gained by producing these locomotives greatly influenced the construction of the English Electric Class 40 diesels and the 'Peaks'. *Colour-Rail*

Right:
The third of the Bulleid designed diesel-electric express locomotives, No 10203, which was built at Brighton, did not enter service until 1954. This locomotive was fitted with the 16SVT MkII engine rated at 2,000bhp at 850 rpm, thereby making its performance far superior to the earlier pair. It was considered to be powerful enough to cope with the 'Royal Scot' without assistance and was also used on 'Golden Arrow' and 'Night Ferry' trains in 1955. No 10203 did not have a gangway to enable working in multiple. No 10203 is pictured in black livery, with silver bogies, on a test train at Waterloo in April 1954.
The Late S. C. Townroe/Colour-Rail DE629

Left:
In 1941, the first of the Bulleid/Raworth 1,470hp Co-Co electric locomotives, No CC1, appeared out of Ashford Works. The locomotive could pick up the electric current from the third-rail or by the use of a centrally-fitted pantograph from overhead current. This locomotive was originally numbered in the Bulleid tradition of 'C' denoting a six-wheel bogie, of which there were two, and '1' denoting the first in the class. BR numbered the locomotive 20001 and, carrying this number when sporting the BR blue livery, this locomotive is seen at St James's Bridge, East Croydon, on 31 May 1968, with a Royal Train for Tattenham Corner.
C. J. Gammell

Above right:
The second of Bulleid's Co-Co electric locomotives, No CC2, did not emerge until 1943. This locomotive regularly worked the London Victoria to Newhaven boat trains. Both Nos CC1 and CC2 were often called upon to work Royal Trains. Although many modifications were carried out on No CC2, externally this locomotive looked similar to the first member of the class. Multiple-unit jumpers were also added to the front end of No CC2. In 1948, No CC2 was painted light blue/grey with silver lining along the top. In fact, this was a proposed colour scheme for all BR electric locomotives. In this view at Eastleigh in September 1964, No CC2 (now 20002) sports the green livery with white roof, having just emerged from the paint shop.
The Late B. J. Swain/Colour-Rail

Below right:
The last of the Bulleid/Raworth-designed electric locomotives did not appear until 1948 and was numbered 20003. This locomotive was even more box-like in appearance with a front similar to a '4SUB' unit. The pantograph on all three locomotives enabled safer operations in goods yards for the staff and a number of yards on the SR were equipped with lightweight catenary for the purpose. No 20003 could regularly be seen at Three Bridges, as in this view of 16 March 1963. All three of these Bulleid electric locomotives were reliable and they lasted in service until 1969. They were only withdrawn at that time because they were 'non-standard'. *Geoff Rixon*

Left:

To emphasise the popularity of the Bulleid Pacific — and the fact that many reached the famous scrapyard at Barry — there are 10 air-smoothed versions preserved, 10 rebuilt 'West Country/Battle of Britain' Pacifics and 11 rebuilt 'Merchant Navy' 4-6-2s. Wherever you go in Britain to visit railway preservation sites it is almost guaranteed that you will see one of Bulleid's Pacific locomotives. Of the unrebuilt versions, only one carries the original Southern Railway number. This is 'West Country' No 21C123 *Blackmore Vale* which, like most preserved locomotives, is seen in immaculate condition sporting the Malachite Green livery as it nears Freshfield Halt on the Bluebell Railway on 14 June 1981.
Hugh Ballantyne

Above:

To the delight of all steam enthusiasts, the Southern Bulleid Pacifics move from one preserved site to the next on a regular basis. The unrebuilt 'West Country' No 34105 *Swanage* was performing well on the Mid-Hants Railway in the spring of 1992 and, on 19 April of that year, it was seen climbing Medstead Bank with the 10.40 train from Alresford to Alton. This line, with its steep inclines, is a real test for all locomotives.
Hugh Ballantyne

Below:
A particularly exciting sight for the steam enthusiast of today is to see main-line running, and these well-patronised trains also generate a flood of lineside photographers and onlookers. Of the many special trains hauled by main-line steam, one of the most impressive is the 'Cumbrian Mountain Express', and the lineside of the Settle & Carlisle line when one of these trains is due is scattered with enthusiasts. In this view of 29 May 1982, unrebuilt 'West Country' Pacific No 34092 *City of Wells* is seen near Long Preston on one of these specials. This locomotive was first named *Wells* in November 1949 and was renamed *City of Wells* in March 1950. *C. J. Gammell*

Right:
Carrying appropriate embellishments for a 'West Country' Pacific but in the wrong part of the country, No 34092 *City of Wells* creates a Christmas card scene as it sits near the the huge coaling tower at Carnforth shed in December 1981, as the day draws to a close. *Geoff Rixon*

Left:
To some enthusiasts who remember the halcyon days of steam on BR, the sight of a Southern locomotive on a LMS or LNER line takes a little getting used to and many prefer, as far as possible, locomotives that once worked those lines to again appear on them in their preserved state. But this is not a perfect world and the sight of any fine steam locomotive in action is a welcome one. In September 1991, unrebuilt 'Battle of Britain' Pacific No 34072 *257 Squadron* was in use on the North Yorkshire Moors Railway. As it pounded up the steep incline into Goathland from Grosmont, the sight of the locomotive would have impressed any North Eastern steam enthusiast. After a stop a Goathland, No 34072 is pictured making a spirited departure from the station with a train for Pickering. The locomotive is seen carrying the Ian Allan *Railway World* headboard. *Rex Kennedy*

Right:
Only one member of the Bulleid 'Q1' 0-6-0 class is preserved — No 33001. This locomotive can now be seen in action on the Bluebell Railway. On 3 January 1993, when the snow was deep and crisp and even, this winter wonderland scene was captured as the 'Q1' is helped by the cold conditions to provide an impressive smoke effect when seen at West Hoathly on this popular preserved railway. *C. J. Gammell*

Left:
Since the demise of main-line steam there have been a number of spectacular events to celebrate particular anniversaries. Most notably these included the Shildon exhibition of 1975, which marked the 150th anniversary of the Stockton & Darlington Railway, and Rainhill in 1980, which celebrated the opening in 1830 of the Liverpool & Manchester Railway. Both of these events provided an excellent steam spectacle. Rebuilt 'Merchant Navy' Pacific No 35028 *Clan Line* is seen providing an attraction for the Southern enthusiasts at Rainhill. Sporting its 'Golden Arrow' embellishments and literally 'waving the flag', *Clan Line* puts on an excellent display for the onlookers on 24 May 1980. Sadly Rainhill was not as well patronised as the event five years earlier at Shildon. *C. J. Gammell*

Above:
From the early days of main-line steam running in Britain by preserved locomotives, 'Merchant Navy' Pacific No 35028 *Clan Line* has always been a crowd puller and, in this scene of 29 August 1988, this locomotive is seen with the 'Shakespeare Limited'. The train had started from Marylebone station and has been captured at South Hampstead crossing the West Coast main line with its well-patronised special.
C. J. Gammell

Left:
Rebuilt 'West Country' Pacific No 34027 *Taw Valley* is a comparative newcomer to the preserved scene and is a welcome sight on main-line steam runs. On 23 July 1989, it was the motive power for the 'North Wales Coast Express' from Holyhead to Crewe, a train which helped bring steam back to the North Wales main line. It is seen arriving at Llandudno Junction from Llandudno and this scene captures the dramatic backdrop of Conwy Castle as the train heads back to England.
Hugh Ballantyne

Above:
Also in 1989, preserved rebuilt 'West Country' No 34027 *Taw Valley* was used on the Severn Valley Railway and, on 24 September of that year, the locomotive approaches Bewdley tunnel with empty coaching stock from Bridgnorth for Kidderminster. One cannot appreciate the hours of hard labour put in by enthusiasts to bring these locomotives back to life. There is no praise high enough for these hard working enthusiasts.
Hugh Ballantyne

When preservation first started taking shape, one would visit preservation sites and would often wonder if trains would ever run over their stretches of track. However, today most have revenue-earning trains and represent some of the best tourist attractions that Britain can offer. For anyone who saw 'Merchant Navy' Pacific No 35005 *Canadian Pacific* rotting away amongst the lines of locomotives in Barry Docks in the late 1960s and early 1970s, it would not have been thought pos-

sible for this locomotive to rise from the grave. But here we see *Canadian Pacific* in all her glory, on 4 May 1991, as it crosses Swithland Viaduct with the 13.00 Loughborough to Rothley train on the Great Central Railway. *Hugh Ballantyne*

Below:
Of course, for the true Southern enthusiast, there is no finer sight than that of a Bulleid Pacific on Southern metals and, on 21 June 1992, preserved 'West Country'

Pacific No 34027 *Taw Valley* was back at Yeovil Junction with the NSE tour to Exeter Central, proudly sporting the 'Atlantic Coast Express' headboard. Let us hope that for years to come we shall continue to witness Oliver Bulleid's fine machines, and their rebuilds, putting in sterling performances over Britain's main lines and at the many preservation sites, as this is a part of Britain's railway history which must continue into the next century. *Hugh Ballantyne*

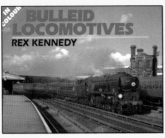